My Home in the City

Miranda Kelly

CRABTREE
PUBLISHING COMPANY
WWW.CRABTREEBOOKS.COM

My home in the **city**.
What can we do?

We can play at the **park**.

We can go to the **zoo**.

My city is big.
Sometimes it's **loud**.

9

My mom makes sure I'm never lost in the **crowd**.

My home in the city.
We walk to the store.

We lunch on a bench.
We can do so much more.

Let's visit my **friends**.
They live on my street.

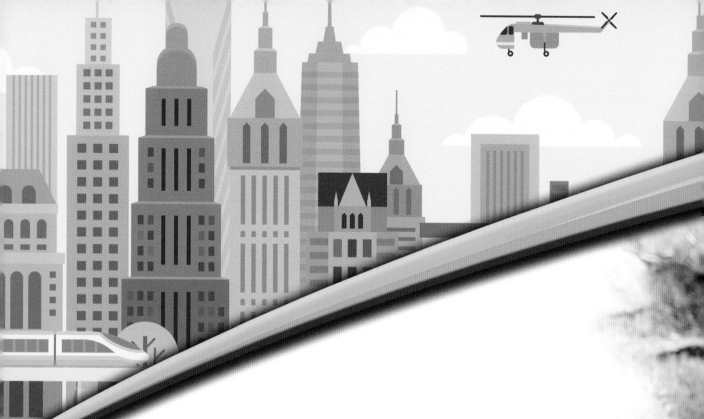

After school is a good time to meet.

I love my home in the city.

Glossary

 **city** (SIT-ee): A city is a place where people live and work. A city is bigger than a town.

 **crowd** (KROUD): A crowd is a large group of people.

 **friends** (FRENDZ): Friends are the people you like to spend time with.

 **loud** (LOUD): When something is loud, it makes a lot of sound. A city is loud.

park (PARK): A park is a place that has trees and benches. Some parks have a playground.

zoo (ZOO): A zoo is a place where animals are kept for people to see.

Index

School-to-Home Support for Caregivers and Teachers

Crabtree Seedlings books help children grow by letting them practice reading. Here are a few guiding questions to help the reader with building his or her comprehension skills. Possible answers are included.

Before Reading

- What do I think this book is about? I think this book is about a home in a city.

- What do I want to learn about this topic? I want to learn about activities that people can do in the city.

During Reading

- I wonder why... I wonder why the city is loud. Where do the loud sounds come from?

- What have I learned so far? I have learned that people in cities can play at the park and go to the zoo.

After Reading

- What details did I learn about this topic? I learned that many people in cities walk from place to place.

- Read the book again and look for the vocabulary words. I see the word ***crowd*** on page 10 and the word ***friends*** on page 16. The other vocabulary words are found on pages 22 and 23.

Library and Archives Canada Cataloging-in-Publication Data

Title: My home in the city / by Miranda Kelly.
Names: Kelly, Miranda, 1990- author.
Description: Series statement: In my community | "A Crabtree seedlings book". | Includes index.
Identifiers: Canadiana 20200388142 |
  ISBN 9781427129567 (hardcover) |
  ISBN 9781427129666 (softcover)
Subjects: LCSH: City and town life—Juvenile literature.
Classification: LCC HT152 .K45 2021 | DDC j307.76—dc23

Library of Congress Cataloging-in-Publication Data

Names: Kelly, Miranda, 1990- author.
Title: My home in the city / by Miranda Kelly.
Description: New York, NY : Crabtree Publishing Company, [2021]
| Series: In my community : a Crabtree seedlings book |
Includes index. Identifiers: LCCN 2020050775 |
  ISBN 9781427129567 (hardcover) |
  ISBN 9781427129666 (paperback)
Subjects: LCSH: City and town life--Juvenile literature.
Classification: LCC HT152 .K45 2021 | DDC 307.76--dc23
LC record available at https://lccn.loc.gov/2020050775

Crabtree Publishing Company
www.crabtreebooks.com 1-800-387-7650
e-book ISBN 978-1-947632-64-6
Print book version produced jointly with Crabtree Publishing Company NY, USA

Written by Miranda Kelly
Production coordinator and Prepress technician: Amy Salter
Print coordinator: Katherine Berti

Printed in the U.S.A./012021/CG20201112

Photo credits: City illustration © avian; Cover and page 2-3 © shutterstock.com/IM_photo; page 4-5 © shutterstock.com/Olga Enger; page 6-7 © shutterstock.com/FamVeld; page 8-9 © shutterstock.com/Tupungato; page 10-11 © shutterstock.com/Alex Brylov; page 12-13 © shutterstock.com/Ryan DeBerardinis; page 14-15 © shutterstock.com/Tatiana Bobkova; page 16-17 © shutterstock.com/Africa Studio; page 18-19 ©istock.com/ Stock Photos | Education Building; page 20-21 ©istock.com/SeanPavonePhoto

Published in Canada
Crabtree Publishing
616 Welland Ave.
St. Catharines, ON
L2M 5V6

Published in the United States
Crabtree Publishing
347 Fifth Ave
Suite 1402-145
New York, NY 10016

Published in the United Kingdom
Crabtree Publishing
Maritime House
Basin Road North, Hove
BN41 1WR

Published in Australia
Crabtree Publishing
Unit 3 – 5
Currumbin Court
Capalaba QLD 4157